you
choose

you
choose

a handbook for

staff working

with people

who have

learning disabilities

to promote

self-esteem and

self-advocacy

jenny mosley

Pavilion
PUBLISHING

you choose

a handbook for staff working with people who have
learning disabilities to promote self-esteem and self-advocacy

Jenny Mosley

Published by:

Pavilion Publishing (Brighton) Limited
8 St George's Place
Brighton
East Sussex BN1 4GB
Telephone 01273 623222
Fax 01273 625526
Email pavpub@pavilion.co.uk

A catalogue record for this book is available from The British Library.

First published by LDA, Cambridge, 1994.

(ISBN 185503 2023)

Republished by Pavilion, 1997

ISBN 1 900600 45 1

Printing: Ashford Press (Southampton)

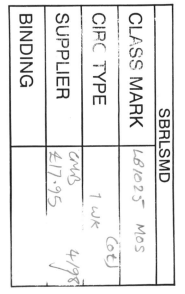

Contents

Acknowledgements

The Writers Group

Hazel Cheesman	*– instructor at day centre*
Sara Crowley	*– social worker with community living team*
Andy Day	*– residential worker*
Ronnie Hedge	*– instructor at day centre*
Kim Holmes	*– social worker*
Wendy Joslin	*– instructor at day centre*

We would like to thank all the people we worked with, for contributing their ideas and for being willing to explore new ideas with us. In particular we would like to thank the following people who came from one of the day centres and joined the Writers Group on one of their writing days.

Philip Barwell

Nichola Grant

Howard Murphy

We are all greatly appreciative of the efforts of Sue Wood, the staff development and training officer for Wiltshire Social Services who had the vision and energy to find ways to support this writing project.

Jenny Mosley

A book about advocacy: why now?

> 'Care management establishes a climate in which representation and advocacy can flourish. Local authorities are positively encouraged to promote the development of local advocacy schemes.'
>
> *CARE MANAGEMENT AND ASSESSMENT – PRACTICE GUIDANCE 1991*

> 'The individual service user and normally, with his or her agreement, any carers should be involved throughout the assessment and care management process.'
>
> *CARING FOR PEOPLE – POLICY GUIDANCE 1990*

This is just the right time for a book on advocacy. From everywhere we are being bombarded with exhortations to 'listen to customers', 'identify needs', 'be consumer led not service led', 'empower people,' etc. All absolutely right, but a whole lot easier to say than to do.

This book offers a wealth of practical advice and suggestions for ways in which we co-workers can really help those we work with to make their own choices and decisions. It will be valuable to all staff or workers who in their work with people with learning disabilities are genuinely trying to make a reality of 'user empowerment'.

Sue Wood
Staff development and training officer

The background 'story' to this book

My own involvement with adults with learning disabilities initially came through my early work as a drama therapist and counsellor. The power of these two therapies to help people reach their inner feelings, surprise themselves and others with their hidden talents, and express themselves in a variety of ways was a most exciting experience for me. My parallel work as a training consultant involved me in the research and exploration of ways to develop self-esteem and I became fascinated by the positive effects that participation in self-esteem programmes had for many adults and children.

Later, further research into current developments in the self-advocacy movement revealed that the many approaches I was now promoting in my own freelance work had much in common with core ideas embedded in self-advocacy.

My initial training had built my commitment to the promotion of active experiential approaches in group work, so when I later ran a series of courses organised by Sue Wood, a training officer for Wiltshire Social Services, on the theme of self-advocacy, I invited a group with learning disabilities from the community care day-centre I was working in, to contribute to the staff training days. Their contribution, focusing on the benefits of group work in their lives, was inspiring and gave all the course workers, trainers and social workers the enthusiasm to want to explore more ways of promoting self-advocacy in their own work situations.

Sue Wood then made the splendid decision that this surge of energy and enthusiasm deserved the training department's backing. After she had mustered the necessary agreements for resources, I agreed to lead an action research writing project. This meant that I would lead a group of staff, all working with people who had learning disabilities, to help them (and myself) to examine our daily work practices and research new ways of working through regular writing and consultation meetings which lasted over a year.

This book chronicles our personal efforts to think about self-advocacy and to promote it in our own work places. It is a highly personal account. We are not claiming to be academic theorists, but people struggling to marry our practice with a hard-earned, rough-edged philosophy.

We analysed our activities critically in the work place. We canvassed for ideas from the people we worked with, we tried new strategies and approaches in our own groups and then returned to our Writers Group to debate with and challenge each other. We invited some service users from our work places to work with us and tell us what they would like included in the book. Their ideas were an enormous help.

The whole project was often an uncomfortable journey. Many times we became frustrated and angry with our own prejudices and limitations, but the discussions were always heartening and supportive. Our hardest job was to actually tear ourselves away from the benefits of talking and put pen to paper!

Jenny Mosley

Self-advocacy and self-esteem

At the outset we were anxious that the term 'self-advocacy' might be yet another jargon term championing a self-evident truth. We were not sure if it had any real significance for us in the way we worked with people with learning disabilities. Searching through the literature on self-advocacy we found that definitions agreed that self-advocates were people who felt able to stick up for themselves, in order to urge others to take into account the choices and decisions they wished to make. So either verbally or non-verbally, a self-advocate is someone who can get her/his message across in order to effect positive changes in her/his life.

This line of thought brought us sharply up against the paradox that in order to be a self-advocate, a person must have some sense of self. A sense of self, more commonly termed self-esteem, is the value or worth we attribute to the picture we have built up of ourselves. This picture comes from the positive and negative responses we have encountered from the people who are important to us.

Many of our clients had already suffered frequent negative and disempowering experiences in their lives which had chipped away at their self-esteem. Clearly, as people wanting to promote self-advocacy, we needed to accept a direct and inescapable link between self-esteem and self-advocacy.

We then wondered if perhaps clients, who responded to our frequent questions regarding their needs or choices by saying, 'Oh, everything is fine, I like it here just as it is,' were really saying, 'My experiences have taught and are still teaching me that it is not safe to have views, let alone express them. If you want me to be a good self-advocate and express my opinions, fight for justice and challenge authority, you will have to prove to me that you are trustworthy. I need to be able to rely on you to stay with this process, be patient and role-model all the qualities you want me to have. And don't forget, I've lost touch with me so help me find a way to the person I am and can be.'

What is good self-esteem?

Good self-esteem is the ability:

◆ to think positively about your qualities

◆ to recognise and develop your unique strengths

◆ to be prepared to work on any weaknesses

◆ to create some success in your life

◆ to do things just for your own pleasure

◆ to accept failure and mistakes without being devastated

◆ to keep all ups and downs in perspective

◆ to find an image you like and are comfortable with

◆ to develop warm, understanding relationships

◆ to recognise and draw out the positive qualities in others without feeling threatened.

What is self-advocacy?

Self-advocacy is the ability:

◆ to stick up for yourself

◆ to say 'No' or 'Yes' because you want to

◆ to make sure that people know what you think

◆ to know your rights as a human being

◆ to get hold of any information you need in order to make decisions

◆ to make choices and carry them out despite setbacks

◆ to try again if you make a mistake

◆ to insist you are treated with respect.

Conclusion

Self-esteem will lead to good self-advocacy.
Self-advocacy will lead to good self-esteem.

Good self-esteem
Good self-advocacy
Good self-esteem
Good self-advocacy

The following diagrams are an attempt to illustrate the reciprocal nature of the link between self-esteem and self-advocacy.

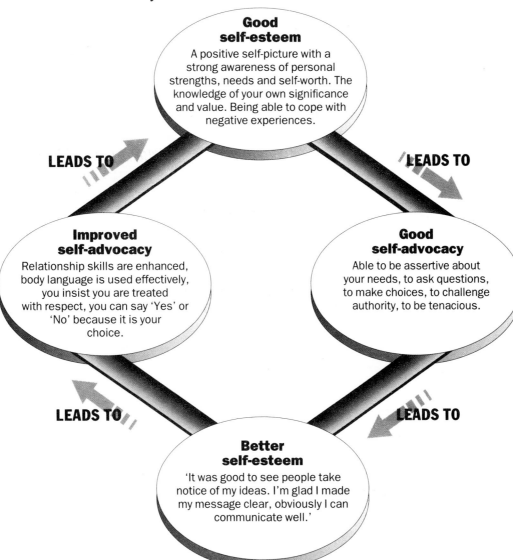

Good self-esteem
A positive self-picture with a strong awareness of personal strengths, needs and self-worth. The knowledge of your own significance and value. Being able to cope with negative experiences.

LEADS TO

LEADS TO

Improved self-advocacy
Relationship skills are enhanced, body language is used effectively, you insist you are treated with respect, you can say 'Yes' or 'No' because it is your choice.

Good self-advocacy
Able to be assertive about your needs, to ask questions, to make choices, to challenge authority, to be tenacious.

LEADS TO

LEADS TO

Better self-esteem
'It was good to see people take notice of my ideas. I'm glad I made my message clear, obviously I can communicate well.'

Poor self-esteem
Poor self-advocacy
Poor self-esteem
Poor self-advocacy

Poor self-esteem
A negative self-picture, little awareness of personal strengths and needs, low self-worth, feeling of insignificance and inability to cope with negative experiences.

LEADS TO

LEADS TO

Reinforced poor self-advocacy
Relationship skills are eroded, diminished ability to command respect and say 'Yes' or 'No' because it is your choice. More likely to 'suffer' unsatisfactory conditions in life.

Poor self-advocacy
Unable to be assertive about your needs, fear of failure, lack of confidence to challenge authority or to ask questions, easily deterred.

LEADS TO

LEADS TO

Reinforced poor self-esteem
'No one takes any notice of me or of what I want. I can't communicate or stand up for myself.'

Implications for staff

It is important that as staff we understand the need to achieve good self-esteem. To feel recognised, significant, worthwhile and respected is a basic human requirement.

Psychologists' research in this field indicates that because of the self-esteem motive people are driven to seek recognition in all sorts of ways. Clients with learning disabilities are particularly disadvantaged and disempowered by society's attitudes towards them. It is important that people working with those who have learning disabilities look after and meet their own need for self-esteem in all areas of their lives.

A commitment to the building of staff self-esteem is vital. Otherwise, being human and fragile, workers will seek to enhance their own self-esteem to the detriment of their clients' self-esteem.

A commitment to the promotion of self-advocacy means that clients must have the opportunity to experience their personal power through empowering relationships that allow them to risk making their own decisions and choices.

What a commitment to self-advocacy began to mean to us as workers

In order to avoid the 'them and us' mentality ('self-advocacy is for clients, we're beyond that'), we needed to make sure that we understood what self-advocacy meant to us in our personal and professional lives. We needed to think about how good we were at promoting our own opinions and needs and how good our colleagues were at dealing with our own attempts at self-advocacy. This lead us to identify a number of prerequisites if we were genuinely commiting ourselves to promoting self-advocacy, both in our lives and the lives of our clients. These are summarised below:

◆ To examine the policy and practice of our establishments with the help of the clients to see if they were really open to exploring personal and professional change as a result of clients' expressed needs.

◆ To constantly examine our adherence to the aim of respect for individuals, ensuring that we were carrying this out in our everyday interactions with everyone we came into contact with.

◆ To sharpen up our observation and listening skills in order to understand the different methods of communication that people use. This would involve us in concerted efforts to explore alternatives to verbal language.

◆ To foster our own self-esteem and actively enhance the self-esteem of our colleagues, to avoid the danger of us abusing our position with clients as a way of making ourselves feel more powerful.

◆ To accept that there would be occasions when we would have to have the courage of our convictions and persevere for a satisfactory or acceptable outcome.

◆ To be prepared to help people use the complaints procedure and Resource Deficiency Form, and in some cases, overcome our fears about them.

◆ To share with both colleagues and clients any information that could help us to promote positive changes.

◆ To accept that the promotion of self-advocacy within our work place might involve all-round change and the need for a system which is able to collect and collate requests for change from individuals and groups, such as regular meetings between members of the management teams and the clients.

◆ To follow a process of self-evaluation in order to monitor our own responses and to avoid simply promoting our own ideas and opinions.

◆ To follow a plan of personal development to ensure that we too were able to understand the benefits of self-advocacy and what sort of setbacks might be encountered in promoting this process within our work places.

◆ To know that as staff we were valued and listened to, and that systems had been created to enhance staff-esteem, for example the formation of staff issues/peer support groups.

Am I a good self-advocate?

It is vital to understand that advocacy is a process of self-development that we are all involved in. Too often we tend to distance ourselves from the client's needs, failing to appreciate that we have the same needs. There is something wrong about service-providers promoting self-advocacy for service-users when they have avoided facing up to their own issues or lack of skills, that are holding them back from being their own self-advocates. Until we can fully appreciate the problems, dilemmas and skills needed to 'stick up' for ourselves we will not be able to help others effectively.

		Yes	No
1	Do I tend to avoid situations or people because I get embarrassed?	☐	☐
2	Do I easily 'fly off the handle'?	☐	☐
3	Do I find it difficult to return goods I am not satisfied with?	☐	☐
4	Do I feel too shy or nervous to put my views/ideas forward in discussions?	☐	☐
5	Do I find criticism very upsetting? Can I cope with making a mistake?	☐	☐
6	Do I rarely stand up for myself against unfair criticism?	☐	☐
7	Do I find it hard to say 'No' to unreasonable demands?	☐	☐
8	If someone makes a racist/sexist comment or joke that offends me, do I find it difficult to challenge?	☐	☐
9	Do I try to 'disappear' at social gatherings?	☐	☐
10	Would I find it difficult to put myself forward for promotion at work?	☐	☐

		Yes	No
11	Would I find it difficult to stand up to my manager if s/he was treating me unfairly?	☐	☐
12	Would I find it difficult to challenge a colleague who was not pulling her/his weight at work, thereby making extra work for me?	☐	☐
13	Do I find it difficult to ask for help or a favour from colleagues?	☐	☐
14	Do I find it hard to initiate conversations with strangers?	☐	☐
15	Do I feel embarrassed about accepting praise?	☐	☐
16	Do I find it hard to express my true feelings?	☐	☐
17	Do I find it difficult to show affection to others?	☐	☐
18	Do I find it difficult to challenge a colleague about her/his negative attitude towards clients?	☐	☐
19	Do I tend to grumble to colleagues about a work problem, rather than approaching the manager directly?	☐	☐
20	Do I meekly accept queue jumpers?	☐	☐
21	Would I ignore blatant anti-social behaviour?	☐	☐
22	Do I allow others to make decisions for me?	☐	☐
23	Do I find it difficult to maintain eye contact when in conversation with others?	☐	☐
24	Would I find it difficult to remind a friend/colleague that s/he owes me money?	☐	☐
25	Would I find it difficult to chase a colleague for overdue work?	☐	☐
26	Do I have difficulty in praising others?	☐	☐
27	Do I often feel resentful about the way I am treated at work?	☐	☐
28	Do I raise my voice or dominate conversation in order to get my point across?	☐	☐
29	Do I have trouble accepting that my opinions are as valid as other people's?	☐	☐
30	Would I resort to 'underhand' methods to try to ensure that my ideas are accepted?	☐	☐

If you found yourself ticking mostly 'Yes' boxes, then you need to spend some time exploring how you can best develop communication skills in your everyday life. Developing communication skills helps us to become confident self-advocates. If you find it difficult to express yourself directly and clearly, then you will be able to appreciate the task facing your clients. This understanding will help you to work harder to create the positive relationships people need to use their own developing advocacy skills.

Remember   It is much harder to be a self-advocate when there is a risk that:
- there will be a backlash later
- someone may laugh at you
- you will be punished later
- an argument might ensue
- someone may get angry
- someone may say something about you behind your back.

Remember   To encourage self-advocacy in others you need to be able to:
- wait patiently until people have had their say
- control your temper or irritability
- remain non-defensive when you are criticised
- carry on offering a positive relationship even if you are hurt by someone else's decision
- think carefully about your powerful persuasion skills, before turning on someone who has said, 'No'.

Above all, it is crucial to check whether any of your responses are disempowering others.

Disempowerment

Clients and staff

Many of life's experiences disempower people, and at one time or another many of us have suffered from other people's disabling attitudes towards us. Our clients, in addition to being hurt by the usual negativity of careless words, also suffer a labelling process that has brought them to our establishments and many have then fallen prey to a prolonged disempowering process.

Much has been written about the complex political and personal process of disempowerment, but it is worthwhile highlighting certain aspects of this process here in order to check we are not contributing to, and perpetuating, the vicious cycle.

A model of disempowerment

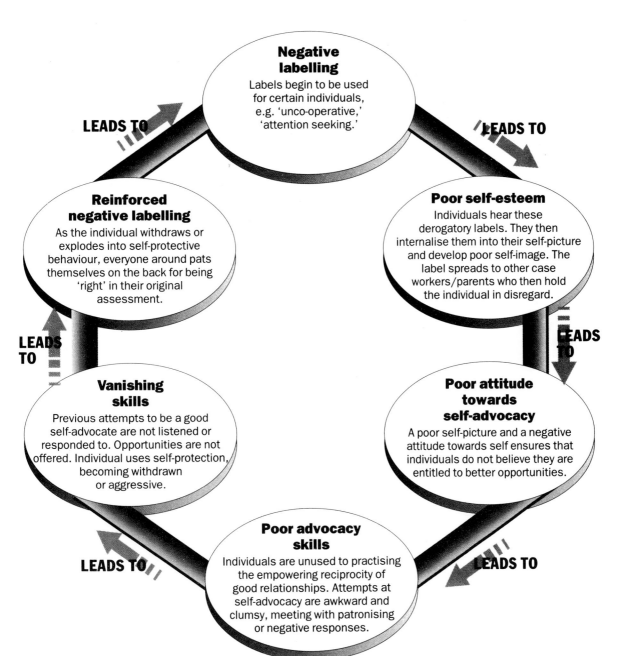

Negative labelling
Labels begin to be used for certain individuals, e.g. 'unco-operative,' 'attention seeking.'

LEADS TO

LEADS TO

Reinforced negative labelling
As the individual withdraws or explodes into self-protective behaviour, everyone around pats themselves on the back for being 'right' in their original assessment.

Poor self-esteem
Individuals hear these derogatory labels. They then internalise them into their self-picture and develop poor self-image. The label spreads to other case workers/parents who then hold the individual in disregard.

LEADS TO

LEADS TO

Vanishing skills
Previous attempts to be a good self-advocate are not listened or responded to. Opportunities are not offered. Individual uses self-protection, becoming withdrawn or aggressive.

Poor attitude towards self-advocacy
A poor self-picture and a negative attitude towards self ensures that individuals do not believe they are entitled to better opportunities.

LEADS TO

LEADS TO

Poor advocacy skills
Individuals are unused to practising the empowering reciprocity of good relationships. Attempts at self-advocacy are awkward and clumsy, meeting with patronising or negative responses.

A model of disempowerment

Example 1

Negative labelling

'People with learning disabilities cannot occupy themselves. They need to be entertained (e.g. TV, bingo). We'll make sure we entertain them as often as we can.'

LEADS TO

LEADS TO

Reinforced negative labelling

Individual withdraws and does not make requests. Workers feel reassured that their original assessment has been confirmed and consider that the individual seems 'happy enough'.

Poor self-esteem

'I need to be with other people. I can't do anything on my own. I get bored unless the TV is on. I'm not good at generating or pursuing my own interests.'

LEADS TO

LEADS TO

Vanishing skills

Skills of independence and creativity (e.g. organisation, preparation and evaluation) diminish. Subsequent anti-social behaviour reflects individual's frustration.

Poor attitude towards self-advocacy

'There's no point in me asking to do something different. I don't want to upset the others watching TV.

Poor advocacy skills

That individual is not then used to practising the skills of independence or creativity. Any attempt at independence fails, which is then seen by others as evidence that the individual cannot function on her/his own.

LEADS TO

LEADS TO

A model of disempowerment

Example 2

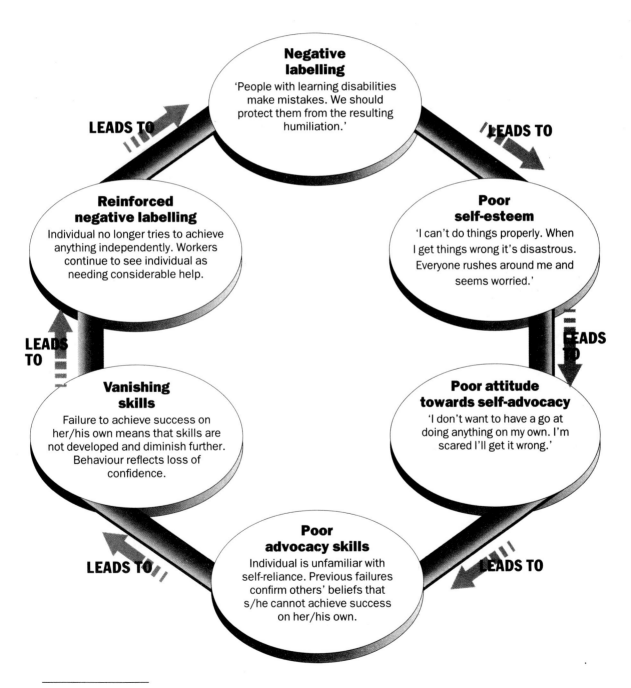

Negative labelling
'People with learning disabilities make mistakes. We should protect them from the resulting humiliation.'

LEADS TO

Poor self-esteem
'I can't do things properly. When I get things wrong it's disastrous. Everyone rushes around me and seems worried.'

LEADS TO

Poor attitude towards self-advocacy
'I don't want to have a go at doing anything on my own. I'm scared I'll get it wrong.'

LEADS TO

Poor advocacy skills
Individual is unfamiliar with self-reliance. Previous failures confirm others' beliefs that s/he cannot achieve success on her/his own.

LEADS TO

Vanishing skills
Failure to achieve success on her/his own means that skills are not developed and diminish further. Behaviour reflects loss of confidence.

LEADS TO

Reinforced negative labelling
Individual no longer tries to achieve anything independently. Workers continue to see individual as needing considerable help.

LEADS TO

Case studies illustrating the disempowerment model

BRIAN refuses to communicate by using either verbal language or signs, in spite of staff initiatives to encourage him and persuade him to attempt some form of communication. Staff become frustrated and remonstrate with Brian as they feel he is deliberately being unresponsive. Their antipathy causes him to become even more withdrawn. He is often left to his own devices and, as time passes, the staff no longer have any expectations of communication from him. He is written off as a waste of time.

BEN has realised that he can gain people's attention, (albeit negative), by playing the clown. He is frequently reprimanded and told not to be 'silly', but since this is the only behaviour he knows will guarantee him attention, he continues to find other ways to annoy people. He is told off further for being childish, becomes increasingly unhappy and in need of attention. He resorts to even more bizarre behaviour to fulfil that need. He thus confirms people's original labels of 'immature' and 'stupid'.

JAKE often has task-related problems and needs help from other people but is unable to ask for it because he does not have the necessary communication skills. This leads to frustration and he becomes angry, shouting out or throwing things. When he is told off for this behaviour he frequently throws further tantrums and feels great resentment. People around then feel so alienated from him that they don't offer the help he needs.

 **CLARE** is considered awkward and feels that nobody likes her. She is often depressed and moody and is told off for being a 'misery'. She tries to withdraw from social groups but is pressurised to join in. Sensing rejection from the other group members, Clare feels isolated but does not know how to express these feelings. She continues to be labelled 'awkward'.

DARREN exhibits bizarre behaviour and is then given attention. However, because he does not respond quickly to this attention, it is soon withdrawn. He continues to behave 'oddly'. The staff are unsure of how to act and each member tries a different method, so that Darren is faced with inconsistent treatment. This confuses Darren who is as difficult as ever and continues to behave oddly.

Examining
our attitudes

To understand how to work effectively with others we must first understand ourselves. We must acknowledge our own strengths, weaknesses and areas of need.

Whether we like it or not, our choice of occupation gives us power over others. However much we wish to believe that we do not abuse this power, we as staff have learned that this is a constant challenge. We have to do daily battle with ourselves not to make snap judgements, not to be guided by inner prejudices, not to make ourselves feel powerful or important at the expense of others. We have to accept that sometimes, being human, we have failed to win these personal battles!

The world we inhabit, with its superficial values promoted largely through media images has, often without us even realising it, encouraged us to value people who are more attractive, successful, witty people who are 'more' than ourselves. We admire, envy and even fear these people because we recognise their power to either bolster or diminish our self-esteem.

The obverse must also hold true, in that we have been encouraged to devalue people who are 'less' than us, people who are weaker, less attractive and less successful. Indeed, our cultural heritage, the fairy tales and myths of our childhood encourage us to see ugly, clumsy people as stupid and even wicked.

It takes energy and commitment to constantly put aside such conditioning and look beyond the initial poor self-presentation or poor relationship skills of the people we work with, to their unique, but often hidden, strengths and qualities.

People who value themselves are not driven by self-esteem motives to seek more recognition at all costs. If we do not value ourselves and our self-esteem is low, we are a danger to the people we work with. It is all too easy to try to enhance our self-image either by trying to make ourselves needed or by blocking other people's chosen way forward in order to experience a sense of significance.

Catching ourselves out

◆ Do you consider you know what is best for your clients, seeking to control their relationships with other staff and clients?

◆ Do you need your clients to live up to your own standards, i.e., be as clean, orderly and polite as you? If they do not, do you feel they are letting you down and that you are publicly disgraced?

◆ Do you feel your clients are 'less' than other people because they do not look or act like the dynamic or attractive people we sometimes catch ourselves wanting to be?

◆ Do you feel that your clients are constantly at your beck and call, at the ATC or at home, and must respond to your attention as you are such a busy person?

◆ Do you disregard your clients' privacy in ways that you would not find acceptable yourself? E.g., do you always knock on a client's door? Do you enter a client's room without permission? Who invites you into their homes? Do you answer their telephones?

◆ Do you corner clients for breaking rules so that they become angry and frustrated with you and with themselves?

◆ Do you allow your own fear to prevent a client from taking a risk in order to learn or to achieve a goal?

◆ Do you tend to deny any mistakes that you make?

'Yes' answers to these questions indicate that you may be suffering from low self-esteem and are in danger of disempowering your clients in order to enhance your own self-image.

Check your communication skills

◆ Do you look away from people when you speak?

◆ Do you sit positioned away from, or turn away from people while they are speaking?

◆ Do you frown, yawn, or grimace in a distracting way while someone is speaking?

◆ Do you wave your arms about in a confusing way when speaking?

◆ Do you speak too fast or too slowly, too loudly or too softly?

◆ Do you use words people cannot understand?

◆ Do you use an unpleasant tone of voice when you are feeling irritable?

◆ Do you interrupt people in mid-sentence?

◆ Do you intellectualise and over-analyse without being asked?

◆ Do you talk about yourself when it has ceased to be relevant to the person listening?

◆ Do you change the topic under discussion?

◆ Do you use flipcharts when some people may not be able to read?

Check the things you say

That's good.

Because I say so.

You're a nuisance.

Do you think you could do that?

These phrases, if spoken with a negative tone of voice, or body language can easily lower a person's self-esteem.

Go and tell – ?

That's not my problem, I'm afraid.

I've told you about that before.

Why?

Out you go.

Explain that!

What?

You're lazy.

Shut the door on the way out.

I don't think that's right.

Oh, yes.

I'm not going to let you.

No, I'm too busy.

Don't answer back.

Where should you be?

I don't know.

You're wrong.

Don't expect me to help.

Stop acting like a baby.

I didn't say you could do that.

Really?

There's no such thing as can't.

Excuse me!!!!!!

I don't believe you.

Did you?

What are you doing now?

Shut up.

Who invited you?

You're silly.

I don't want to know about that.

Come on, just try.

Empowerment – steps towards self-development

Spiritual needs

Do I know how to practise inner relaxation strategies?

Do I ever explore religions, yoga or meditation?

Do I come into contact with areas of natural beauty?

Emotional needs

Have I friends?

Have I ever developed a relationship?

Can I express my feelings?

Can I cry, shout, laugh in my own home?

Do I have times when people show they love and value me?

Creative needs

Do I ever get opportunities to view beautiful paintings?

Do I get the chance to play with textured materials, to listen and move to music?

Do I get the opportunity to develop creative hobbies?

Do I ever sing freely?

To realise our human potential, we need to look at all areas of life.
Here are some trigger questions to help consideration of the issue.

Physical needs

Do I feel physically safe from harm?

Do I feel fit?

Do I get adequate sleep?

Do I have regular exercise?

Do I have a healthy, well balanced diet?

Do I explore and feel comfortable with my sexuality?

Cognitive needs

Do I get opportunities to think?

Do I get time to think things through, structure ideas and plans?

Do I read books, see stimulating films or plays?

Our theory is that if these questions remain unexplored or the answer is often in the negative, then the self either withdraws into apathy or lethargy, or explodes into angry outbursts.

> *Do the people we work with have the same opportunities to develop these areas of self-potential?*

If people are not offered opportunities to answer 'Yes' to at least one or two of the questions in each area of potential self-development they are being denied their right to fully explore their humanity. Lack of fulfilment creates frustration which can only be expressed by extreme behaviours. Aggressive or withdrawn behaviour signifies unmet needs. Unfortunately, such behaviour provokes further negative responses from more powerful people, leading to even fewer self-development opportunities being offered. The result is that real causes of need or unhappiness are never dealt with.

> *Self-advocacy cannot flourish in someone whose situation denies her/him access to exploring areas of self-fulfilment.*

Empowerment – steps towards self-advocacy

Promoting positive attitudes by disregarding any previous negative labelling

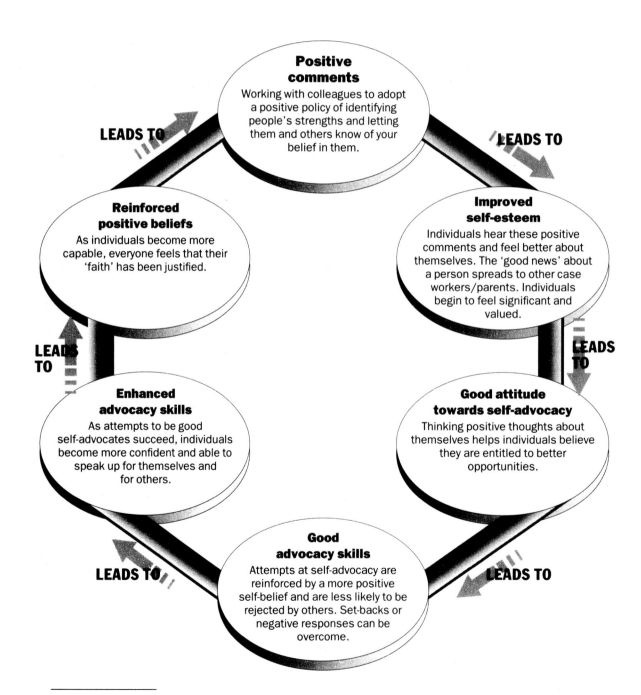

Comments
from clients

Our experience has been that our clients have very clear perceptions of what they want and need in their lives. Below are some examples of these. The wide-ranging nature of their comments illustrates the importance of letting clients speak for themselves rather than imposing our preconceived notions onto them.

> 'I need to receive love, especially from .... Nobody else has really cared for me in the way she has. She makes me feel wanted.'
>
> 'I need people to thank me. When I was at work, my boss wrote a report that showed he appreciated my efforts. If I do a job well, it makes me feel good.'
>
> 'I need to lead an exciting life. I like doing things and don't like it when nothing much happens.'
>
> 'I need to be with people, especially my friends.'
>
> 'I need to be part of people.'
>
> 'I need to relax, especially when I feel I've worked hard. I like to go home and listen to my music. It makes me calm.'
>
> 'I need to help people. I like to see their faces.'
>
> 'I need to know that people trust me.'
>
> 'I need to be on my own sometimes, nice and peaceful.'
>
> 'I need to look good so I wear the right gear. Then people don't look at me and poke fun and I don't feel the odd one out.'
>
> 'I need to be respected by everyone.'
>
> 'I need different things in my job. I'd find it boring to do the same things all day. I need a range of jobs to do.'
>
> 'I need to take part in some exercise like football or swimming.'
>
> 'I need to be good at something and do it really well.'

Personal needs/rights

We found it helpful to think about our 'needs' being our rights.

◆ I have the right to choose to change or not.

◆ I have the right to be talked to properly.

◆ I have the right to be appreciated and thanked for my efforts.

It makes me mad when a person hassles me when I'm trying to do my jobs.

I get really angry when someone doesn't listen and waits until things are bad before talking to me about it.

◆ I have the right to be respected.

◆ I have the right to my own views and opinions.

◆ I have the right to be listened to.

Take us as we are – we're just the same as other people.

◆ I have the right to earn my own money.

◆ I have the right to choose what I spend my money on.

◆ I have the right to make my own choices.

◆ I have the right to be given real responsibility.

◆ I have the right to privacy.

◆ I have the right not to be shouted at.

Talk to us normally, like anyone else.

I hate it when someone acts as if they rule the place.

Don't shout, it frightens me.

Practical initiatives to boost self-esteem in others

- ◆ Be alert and give genuine praise for things done well or that are out of the ordinary.

- ◆ Spend time encouraging people to think of things they do well.

- ◆ Find ways of creating situations where clients assist others, including less able people. There is nothing more disempowering than always being helped.

- ◆ Find ways of enabling people to act independently; e.g., shopping alone, going to the pub with a friend, having a bath, going on holiday or a date, writing a letter, having a Chinese take-away and a bottle of wine.

- ◆ Challenge negative attitudes towards anyone you meet.

- ◆ Spend time with colleagues to help them think about the implications of their work with clients.

- ◆ Go with people at their own pace.

- ◆ Ask for feedback on your own actions ('How do you feel about what we did or what I've just said?'), and act on it!

- ◆ Be genuinely interested by listening and responding with empathy.

- ◆ Encourage self-motivation by getting a client to identify her/his own needs.

- ◆ Help people identify and then reach small targets so they can experience the success and achievement that will motivate them towards the larger challenges.

- ◆ Encourage people to take on specific responsibilities within their homes and work places.

- ◆ Introduce the idea of individual diaries kept by each client, who can ask others to record positive events. This is better than writing notes to send home, as the diary belongs to the individual, who can control what goes in it.

◆ Ask if anyone wants help with their self-image, e.g., clothes, make-up, hairstyle – bring in consultants from outside.

◆ Enhance social skills by organising trips to the theatre, pub, shops etc.

◆ Get together with colleagues and create your own theatre shows – invite the public to watch.

◆ Make it possible for clients to publish a regular newsletter detailing all important events and successes.

◆ Take time to celebrate all successes publicly so the 'good news' spreads.

◆ Work with people towards their chosen goals.

Raising self-esteem – moving towards self-advocacy

Projects we initiated from clients' ideas as steps towards self-advocacy through the building of self-esteem

London in a day

Proposal

A minibus full of people visit London during a normal centre day (9 a.m. – 4 p.m.). The group had not visited the capital before and were not very used to 'different' days without tea breaks, toilets around all the time and everything scheduled.

Anticipated barriers

Some people were worried by the thought of the crowds and the unknown.

Some staff and parents did not think it worthwhile.

Parents thought it would be too tiring.

The risk factor – what if we were late for the buses at 4 p.m.? What if we lost someone?

Recognised benefits

It was for many a totally new experience: a chance to see places only heard of before or seen on television – like Big Ben, Trafalgar Square, mixing with foreigners. All these experiences were exciting and stimulating.

The group really had to work together to make sure there was enough time for shopping and lunch and to get back in time.

Because of the efforts involved, there was a real sense of achievement when the day was a success and everyone was back in time for the bus.

There was a great deal to tell at home afterwards. In many cases people had done something their friends and relations would not attempt.

The main benefit was living up to the expectations of workers. The trip would not have worked without effort and thought by all concerned.

The group wanted to go again and helped to decide where the next trips would be to. In fact, there were six trips in one summer programme and seven in the next year. People continue to talk about them and feel proud of themselves.

Drama

Proposal

A group of people in the Day Centre who had shown interest in drama work before would try to enlist professional help from the local theatre. The aim was to improve the quality of the work done at the Centre by putting on a production for the community.

Anticipated barriers

Not everyone sees drama as important.

Cost of professionals from outside.

Risk of failure, within the group, the Centre and in public.

Concern about participants seeing the value of the project.

Young people from the theatre would be involved. Would their behaviour towards clients be appropriate and vice versa?

Concern that centre staff involved would take on too much extra work at a time when visiting workers were away.

Recognised benefits

A professional approach with high expectations resulted in growth of concentration, responsibility, team work and dedication not often seen in everyday pursuits.

The challenge of the public performances gave everyone more confidence.

The publicity through friends, colleagues, television, radio, newspapers and the theatre's own marketing enhanced feelings of self-worth.

Mixing with young people equally interested in the production built social skills.

Support of 'outsiders' at the theatre felt good.

Individuals' communication skills improved.

The public saw how able many people were.

The shows were highly successful and generally acclaimed.

Adventure

Proposal

To tackle something many people would not dare to do: go up Salisbury Cathedral spire in a builders' lift outside the structure. Many people with learning disabilities also have a physical disability or suffer fits. Consequently many have either not been allowed to do adventurous things, or have been afraid to do so.

Anticipated barriers	Fear of heights.

Fear of the unknown.

Parents' disapproval.

A group outing is not ideal for 'normalisation' in some people's view.

Special arrangements had to be made so that time was allowed for slow movers.

Recognised benefits	People overcame fears.

Exhilaration.

Totally new experience – would encourage more risks.

Gaining admiration of friends, staff and parents.

Completely different view of city and knowledge gained.

Justified self-congratulation.

The experience will be remembered every time the spire is seen.

Sexuality and personal relationships

Proposal

To set up a sexuality and personal relationships group for women. To set up a group climate in which it was safe to discuss issues about sexuality and personal relationships. It would be a forum for discussion, education and support, which would recognise the rights of all people to have relationships with others, including sexual relationships.

Anticipated barriers

Attitudes about people with disabilities not being sexual beings. The group may meet with resistance (from parents, etc.).

The subject may give rise to fear and anxiety in participants and people close to them.

I may have some personal barriers or lack of knowledge on some issues, which might inhibit or effect the way I work.

I may not be supported by colleagues or parents.

Services in the community may not be fully prepared to receive people with disabilities who may need to gain further resources or information.

Much information on the subject is in written form – this is an added handicap to some people's ability to understand.

Recognised benefits	It helped other people consider more carefully their views on disability and sexuality.
	The area of sexuality became a more comfortable, acceptable talking point.
	The group created a forum in which to bring particular concerns.
	People have a greater understanding of their rights.
	People have more knowledge with which they can make informed choices.
	People will practice safer sex.
	People have increased self-awareness and self-esteem.
	People are better prepared for future relationships.
	People have developed confidence in their interactions with others.
What helped	Good supervision for myself.
	The chance to start work with other group leaders.
	To identify and read relevant resource materials.

Outdoor pursuits

Proposal	To set up an outdoor pursuits group for people to experience caving, rock-climbing, canoeing, hill-walking, etc.
	People will be able to take part in activities as part of a group as well as having opportunities for individual achievement.
Anticipated barriers	People underestimating their abilities.
	People may have to overcome fear of water, heights, etc.
	Some people may experience feelings of anxiety.
	Some people may believe that physical limitations inhibit their ability to actively participate.
Recognised benefits	The group allowed people to have fun.
	People were encouraged to be more aware of their senses.
	People were accepted as equal to everyone else.
	People became more confident, which may transfer into other areas of their lives.
	People developed trust of others, and gained others' trust.
	People may develop a new hobby.

The problem-solving goal-achieving group

Personal accounts of groups established in our work places

Several formats were tried for this group, the present one appears to be the most successful. The group begins with a newsround. Everyone is given the opportunity to share some good or bad news with the group. Some people use the time extremely well, others find it difficult to share even the most ordinary experience. No pressure is exerted on those who do not wish to participate. It is hoped that once trust is established they will find the opportunity useful.

When one person is speaking no one else is expected to interrupt, except to ask the speaker a question which is related to what they are talking about. The established pattern is for a volunteer to begin and then we go round the circle in succession. If someone wishes they can 'pass on' to the next person without saying anything. This very rarely happens, people usually want to use the time in some constructive way. People are encouraged to listen actively and ask each other questions.

The next part of the session is used to set achievable goals for that week and to feedback on the progress of past goals.

The achievable goals vary very much from person to person. The ability range is fairly mixed. Time scales are also variable. Some goals are very quickly reached whilst others can take weeks. If this is the case only positive feedback is given and the task may have to be broken down further.

An example   Sarah wanted to break away from her day activity club and enrol at the local College for cookery and computer courses. She felt under pressure to stay at the club because of her ability and sociable nature. She felt she wanted to do something more challenging but was afraid of hurting people's feelings. Making decisions was always difficult for her and she had been 'dithering' for months.

The first goal we set was for her to make a list of the pros and cons. Then she made her own deadline for the final decision. The next goal set was to investigate the practical issues, i.e.: courses, transport, times, cost, who needs to know.

Most of the tasks took just one week to be completed. Others, such as telling those involved, took a little longer. We decided there would be no delay of the final decision date, but the rest of the tasks were flexible. Sarah was quite nervous about telling her club leader so we hit on the idea of mentioning the possibility in casual conversation before going for the 'big one'. When she was ready and had all the above information she felt more confident to broach the subject. In fact she was well ahead of the final date for a decision, but wanted to stick to that. She is now doing both courses and attending the Centre for a drama session. Due to the timing of the cookery course Sarah is able to continue at the club for part of the day anyway!

The quality action group

It was decided to set up a quality action group at the Day Centre. For the first meeting there was a turnout of 52 people interested to find out what it was all about. Not everyone could, or wanted to, make the commitment, but enough people said they would like to form a group to make it viable.

The group stabilised at 23 regular members, 10 of whom were clients. It provided the ideal forum for parents, staff and clients to work together. In order to establish mutual trust and allow all those in the group to work as equals, it was important that the Quality Action Group allowed for everyone to understand all that was said and undertaken.

The Open University Patterns for Living group

This is a course about independent living, relationships and understanding the other person's viewpoint.

A group of six people with learning disabilities studied this course over six months, using the tapes provided, discussion and role-play. As confidentiality was maintained and trust built up, there were some serious and sometimes very personal exchanges. There was also time for listening and being listened to which was extremely valuable. At the end, five out of the six people offered to be co-leaders for the next group to be run.

Listening to other people closely on tape and in person gave many members a way in to discuss deep feelings which normally get pushed away. Having time to explain how their own problems had been tackled in the past, helped others to face their own in the present. Towards the end of the course, life aims were decided. They included:

> to be in a particular TV show
> to act in a show or film
> to make a film
> to do more shopping for oneself
> to take control of personal life
> to climb a mountain
> to be more friendly.

Once these aims had been voiced, the way was clear to achieve some of them, if not all. In fact, the acting and filming opportunities came about through the workshops done with Stage 65, a theatre youth group. The production was in the legitimate theatre and parts of the show, with interviews, went out on television. The person who wanted to film made a video of the show and workshops.

The person who wanted to sort out her own life wanted to leave home. She built up courage, mainly by talking in the group to others who had done it already. She was worried that she would hurt her parents, but when she actually spoke to them they told her that they had not mentioned it before in case she would think they wanted to push her out!

The person who wanted to be 'more friendly' was quite difficult. He did very well in this group, but does not relate easily to many people and when other sessions were not of enough interest to him, he regressed and withdrew again.

The mountain and the shopping were relatively easy things to achieve when discussed at length. The people concerned now know that they can do these things if they really want to, and take the trouble to organise them with friends or staff.

The gardens group

There is a large garden area at the Sarum Centre. Two instructors work with a group of people, some of whom are building up work skills as well as horticultural knowledge. Over the past two years there has been a greater emphasis on selling to the public and working outside the Centre. There are small working parties involved in garden projects in and around Salisbury comprising people working individually in shops and in house gardens.

There have been very successful exhibits at the South of England Flower Show with people running the stall and talking to the public. These very public events give a great boost of confidence and self-esteem, enabling ordinary exchanges and events to be handled with more ease. Working closely with staff means that there is a particular opportunity to be seen as equals.

The individuals feel that:

> *'We make a good team.'*
> *'We like the opportunity to do the stall by ourselves.'*
> *'We feel we got ourselves known and it gave us more confidence to run a stand at another show.'*
> *'We like the way the public speak to us freely.'*

Staff feel that:

> *They have learned to take more risks, to trust in others' abilities.*
> *They have learned to share more. They plan well and feel the benefits.*
> *They have allowed people to take chances, risking mistakes and possibly approbation or even abuse.*

The value of group work

One of the most important ways in which we felt, as staff, we could enhance people's self-esteem was through developing our own group work skills. Many theories of self-esteem point out that if an individual becomes part of a group they trust and feel safe in, then the group can open up to that individual a new, more positive view of their self.

For a self-advocacy group to help people, it must offer a climate of safety in which structures and strategies are introduced to help people express themselves and to explore their creativity.

Some experts say that true self-advocacy means that people with learning disabilities should run their own groups. Whilst this is a laudable ideal, the reality is that running groups involves certain skills that have to be experienced and learned. It is important that staff get training in group work skills first so that they can then pass on these specialised skills to clients who then become more confident and willing to take over later.

Common problems reported by clients in self-advocacy groups

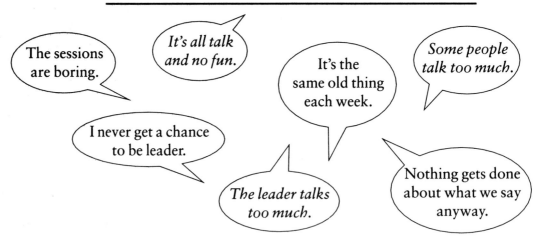

The sessions are boring.

It's all talk and no fun.

It's the same old thing each week.

Some people talk too much.

I never get a chance to be leader.

The leader talks too much.

Nothing gets done about what we say anyway.

What a good group can achieve

◆ It helps people to 'bond', to care about each other.

◆ It generates fun.

◆ It encourages people to take risks.

◆ It provides a safe environment.

◆ It helps people to reach their feelings more easily.

◆ It releases creativity and spontaneity.

◆ It gives people something to look forward to.

◆ It gives people a sense of significance and self-worth.

◆ It helps people to realise ambitions.

◆ It encourages people to set targets.

Applying Maslow's model of needs as a rationale for the value of group work

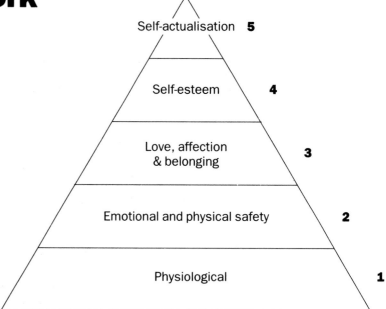

Self-actualisation **5**

Self-esteem **4**

Love, affection & belonging **3**

Emotional and physical safety **2**

Physiological **1**

Stage 1   Sitting in a circle allows everyone to see each other and to pick up non-verbal signs very quickly, e.g., if people are tired or anxious.

Stage 2   Ground rules help people create emotional and physical safety within a group. Trust builds as people adhere to these over a period of time.

Stage 3   Group work promotes a feeling of belonging which generates mutual affection and care.

Stage 4   Being part of a group, having significance and value within that group, enhances people's self-esteem. The group can help people set small realistic targets and then celebrate their success.

Stage 5   Group work provides people with opportunities to try out ideas and encourages them to realise their creative potential within a safe setting. This positive experience can then give them strength to try out a similar creative approach in their daily lives.

Group work skills for leaders

◆ Is there a genuine need for a group?

◆ What type of group would be useful to people?

◆ Is there anything relevant available elsewhere?

◆ Do existing structures allow for a new group?

◆ What are the implications for other staff members?

◆ What are the cost implications?

        to individuals: personal equipment
                                travel
                                contributions;

        to the establishment: staff time
                                    resources
                                  venue
                                  communication.

◆ Will outside help be required by the new group?

What personal communication skills should the group leader possess?

To be able to listen effectively.

To be able to concentrate on another person without being distracted by her/his own thoughts.

To be able to show that all contributions are valued though they may appear irrelevant.

To be able to clarify what people wish to convey.

To achieve good communication it is helpful to:

◆ make good eye contact

◆ lean forward and look interested, smile, nod etc.

◆ use open questions

◆ summarise what you think the person is saying

◆ be aware of disparities between verbal/non-verbal behaviour

◆ make sure everyone has the opportunity to speak

◆ ask for more information

◆ ask for specific examples

◆ repeat key words which the person has used

◆ use people's names

◆ encourage 'silent' members to contribute, perhaps in a 'round'.

Remember not to:

◆ talk too much and monopolise discussion

◆ interrupt people

◆ question in an aggressive manner

◆ misrepresent what people have said.

To become more effective group leaders, individuals will require one or more of the following:

◆ regular supervision

◆ increased opportunities to acquire new skills and ideas

◆ easily accessible resources

- opportunities to replenish personal creativity and reduce any sense of isolation by networking with other group workers

- time to further knowledge of group theory in order to understand group processes.

With this type of support the service offered will be of a better quality and will, in the long term, be more cost effective than a service offered by isolated, stressed staff unable to achieve their potential as group leaders.

Setting up a new group

When setting up any new group it is important to bear in mind certain considerations.

- Establish clear aims and objectives.
- Establish ground rules in the first session (agreed by the whole group.)
- Create structures that maximise participation, e.g., warm-ups, rounds, small groups working within the larger group, working in pairs.

Planning each session beforehand will enable the group workers to ensure that each session has:

a beginning	(creating a safe framework)
a middle phase	(providing relevant and sufficient exercises)
and an ending	(winding down on a positive note).

Each session should have a mixture of discussion and physical activity. The pace of exercises should be appropriate to the needs of individuals within the group, so the leader needs to be aware of the dynamics of the particular group.

Group members should be encouraged to offer both verbal and non-verbal support to other people. The creation of an affirming culture within the group is vital. The philosophy should be one of building and maintaining self-esteem. This may require the inclusion in the ground rules of an 'opt-out clause'.

Styles of group leadership

In order to ensure that a person can fulfil her/his role as group leader certain essential skills are required:

◆ knowledge of group theory
◆ familiarity with methods and techniques of running a group
◆ empathy with other people
◆ respect for other people's views and opinions
◆ confidence in the role as group leader
◆ the ability to enjoy the role and make the other group members feel relaxed.

Three main group leadership styles

Taking a back seat

The leader rarely promotes her/his views, but encourages group members to solve problems between themselves. This allows for creative thinking, but care needs to be taken that the group does not become frustrated and aimless.

Everyone is equal

The leader provides the basic group structure but will conform to meet the group's needs. All group members take part in decision-making. This style gives all members equal power, but unless implemented efficiently, it can lead to the members being unsure about who is in control.

I am in control

The leader provides a firm and definite structure for the group members to follow and controls the content of discussion. Under this style the group members are clear about what is required of them, but it can inhibit some members from contributing.

Beware of the following mistakes:

not allowing enough time for discussion

not listening properly to all group members

allowing one or a few people to dominate discussion.

At the end of the group session it is important to bear the following issues in mind:

some people will have problems parting from the group

what has been learned must relate to the real world

the achievements of the session need clarifying with group members

the group needs to feedback on how they feel about the group and themselves

people should be encouraged to tell each other the positive qualities they have noticed

establish a parting ritual for the end of each session

make sure you find ways, verbal or non-verbal that people can evaluate the group.

Make sure that at the end of the group you have supervision and are able to 'de-brief' properly so you can learn for the future.

Content, ideas, strategies and approaches

Games

These unite groups. They are enjoyable and break down tensions, adding a sense of fun to the group's purpose. They have their own discipline, encouraging self-control and group participation, verbal and physical contact. Many games can be adapted to help people consider abstract concepts, such as trust and co-operation.

Rounds

A theme or idea is selected and everyone takes a turn to speak. For example a sentence is started and each person completes it (I feel happy when ...). Every comment is acceptable and no one can comment on what anyone else says. Group members can say, 'I pass' if they wish. Rounds can be used at any point, when the group needs to hear each others' opinions or wish to evaluate together.

Brainstorming

Ideas are contributed as fast as possible without any prioritising. This emphasises group creativity and the fact that everyone has a valid contribution to make. Ideas are structured later into categories and used as a basis for decision-making.

'Touch' activities

Research shows that touch makes people feel better about themselves. All of us need to be hugged, but if a leader does not feel able to do that then s/he can always shake the person's hands or touch her/his arms.

Talking and listening exercises

These help people to give and receive feedback, based on the 'Lifeskills' model, i.e. 'People who talk to others make friends more easily. If you have a problem you can get help or new ideas by talking it through with someone else. If people tell you what they think of you, it gives you a chance to change if you want... and if you do like what they say it confirms that you are who you think you are...'

Role-play

This helps people to actively engage in what makes sense to them in terms of past experience and present levels of understanding. It enables people to express hidden feelings, discuss problems, practice empathy, try out new behaviour, portray generalised social problems and dynamics of group interaction. It also emphasises the importance of non-verbal emotional response.

Effective de-briefing is vital as some people can find it hard to come out of their role.

Discussion and reflection

Discussion requires the putting forward of more than one point of view. It requires those involved to be prepared to examine and be responsive to the different opinions put forward. It is a deliberate co-operative task which encourages the group to reflect on the meanings underlying their experience.

Sample activities for enhancing self-esteem through group work

All the ideas in the following pages have been tried and tested

Warming-up exercises

1. *Good for* — Relaxation.
Fun.
Becoming a cohesive group.

What to do — Stand in a circle. The leader teaches the group breathing exercises; e.g., slow breaths in, hold, slow breaths out in silence, stand still a few moments.

Variation — As above – with hand on tummy/chest to feel/experience breath.

2. *Good for* — Relaxation.
Fun.
Becoming a cohesive group.

What to do — Stand in a circle. The leader shows the group fast rhythmic breaths in and out. The group follows/joins in.

Variation — Breaths can be slow, depending on the 'feel' of group. With sound. With long, deep breath, and silence and stillness to end.

3. *Good for* — As above.
Voice.
Relaxing inhibition.

What to do — The leader makes sounds, e.g., ah, oh, eee, uugh, sss, sh, mm, la. These are copied.

Variation — The sounds can be varied in volume and length as group dynamics change and people relax.

4. *Good for*   Loosening up physically.
Relaxing.
Fun.
Gives awareness of body ability.

What to do   The leader takes the group through loosening-up exercises, starting with foot-shaking, up through the body – ankle, knees, whole leg, pelvic area, hips, waist, upper torso, upper arms, forearms, whole arm, wrists, fingers, whole hand, shoulders, face (tongue, eyes, jaw), head. Shake everything!

5. *Good for*   Trusting others in group.
Encouraging interaction.

What to do   Touch games. Everyone touches another person in some way. The same parts can be touched, e.g., elbow, hand or knee.

Variation   One person offers to be touched by everyone else at the same time.

6. *Good for*   Warm-up exercises.
Gentle contact.
Group feeling.

What to do   Standing or sitting in a circle, each person gently pats the person in front of them on the back.

7. *Good for*   Relaxation.
Eye contact.

Equipment   Mirrors.

What to do   Everyone looks in a mirror and finds out what colour her/his eyes are. Find someone else with the same eye colour and shake hands. Form groups with other people of same eye colour.

Variation   Extend idea of groups by dividing into smaller groups, with light-dark versions of colours.

Magic islands

Good for Physical contact.
Helping others.

Equipment An 'island' for each group member, e.g., mats, large pieces of paper.
Cassette or record player.
Music cassettes or records.

What to do While the music plays everyone moves around the room. When the music stops people stand on an island. Each time one island is removed. No one is 'out' (as in musical chairs); instead people must fit on fewer islands. Participants join others on an island and help to keep others out of the 'sea'. Eventually everyone is standing on the same island.

A problem solved is a problem shared

Good for Clearing the air before starting a group for anyone feeling worried or anxious.

Giving the group a sense that they have the power to solve problems.

What to do The leader asks the question, 'Does anyone here need help with a problem?' They state, 'I need help because...' The leader explains that any group member can offer help, but only with a sentence starting; 'Would it help if I...?' Would it help if you...?'

Typical requests for help might be:

'I need help with my temper.'
'I need help to join the library.'
'I need help to tie my tie.'
'I need help because I want to...'

The person needing help gives her/his response to the suggestions, e.g.,

'I'm not sure I could do that.'
'I'd be afraid of trying that.'
'I'd like to do that but I'd need my key worker to help me.'

That person then decides what course of action s/he would like to take – the leader jots it down and the following week asks the group member if s/he would like to report back.

If I were...

Good for Helping people to clarify who they are and what they want to be or do.

What to do Examples:

> If I were a building I'd be a .... because ....
> If I were a bird I'd be a .... because ....
> If I were an animal I'd be a .... because ....

Each group member has a turn to complete the statement.

Afterwards any group member may change her/his original idea by saying, 'I'd rather be a .... because ....'

Members are then asked to complete a statement about themselves, what they would like to be or do.

Can you hear me?

Good for Developing listening skills.
Strengthening confidence.
Trusting the group.

What to do Within the circle two people are blindfolded. One person is named 'the hunter' the other as 'the hunted'. The aim of the game is that the hunter should find the hunted by sound alone. People on the outside of the circle guide back, by a gentle touch, anyone who moves too near the circle's edge.

Development When the game is over people talk about what it felt like to rely just on sound. The whole group can talk about sounds they enjoy. Sighted people can each think of something they would miss seeing. Visually impaired people can talk about things they would like to see.

The colour game

Good for
Fun.
Quick thinking.
Visualisation.

What to do
Choose a colour, e.g., red, and say, 'Red is...'
Group members must think of something they associate with red.

e.g.,   'Red is the lounge carpet.'
               'Red is when I'm angry.'
               'Red is a fire.'

Then choose another colour and repeat the process.

Introductions (name game)

Good for
Boosting self-esteem.
Developing concentration and memory.
Getting to know people.

What to do
In a circle, each person says their own name with an alliterative positive describing word, e.g., 'Joyful Janice,' 'Kind Keith'.

Variation
Each person goes around the group to remember all the other people's names. Use an action gesture with the name. Everyone repeats the name with its action.

Getting to know you (name game)

Good for
Building confidence.
Getting to know each other.
Developing observation skills.

What to do
In a group each person says their name and mimes something they enjoy doing. Other people in the group guess the mime and tell the rest of the group.

Variations
The person acts out or mimes a feeling. Others in the group guess the feeling or act it out.

Names chain

Good for Getting to know people.
Quick thinking and speedy reactions.

What to do In a circle, everyone claps their hands on their knees and then claps their hands in a rhythm. The first person says his/her own name and that of someone else in the group, e.g., 'Susan to Paul,' and the next person carries the chain on – 'Paul to Eileen.' The names are said in time with the clapping and after practice the chain of names can be continuous.

Variation Instead of clapping, use a ball to throw around the group, saying the names of the thrower and catcher as you go.

Circle warm-up

Good for Developing trust.
Warming up.
Encouraging safe touch.

What to do The group stands close together in a circle and each person turns to face the back of the person next to her/him. Everyone gently pats the shoulders of the person in front. Everyone turns around to be facing the person on her/his other side and pats her/his shoulders.

Variation Use different techniques, e.g., rubbing, stroking, tapping or touch arms, back, head, neck, or whatever feels comfortable. In the same arrangement, everyone sits on the lap of the person behind. The whole circle of people try to balance in a sitting position.

Feely bag

Good for Developing trust.
Using the sense of touch to recognise textures.
Encouraging safe touch.

Materials A number of opaque bags containing objects of various textures, e.g., gravel, feathers.

What to do	Each person takes a turn in placing her/his hand in the bag and guessing what it is s/he can feel.
Variation	Ask a person to find a particular object by feeling for it. Give congratulations when s/he is successful.

Good touch

Good for	Developing awareness of personal space. Breaking down inhibitions. Encouraging safe touch.
What to do	One person in the group agrees to be 'it'. Other members of the group pat or stroke her/him on the shoulder, arm, back or wherever it feels comfortable.
Variation	The person says whether or not s/he likes the touch and why, e.g., 'I don't like you touching my leg, it feels too intimate.'

People to people

Good for	Developing trust. Practising co-ordination, balance and poise. Encouraging safe touch.
What to do	Group members find a partner. The leader of the group shouts out parts of the body which each partnership are to touch together and then moves on to the next, e.g., 'hands to hands', or 'elbow to back'. When the leader shouts, 'people to people' everyone moves on to find a new partner.

Human knot

Good for	Breaking down inhibitions. Team work. Communication. Encouraging safe touch.

What to do	All the group members huddle together and reach across to link both hands with someone else in the huddle. Then, without breaking the linked hands, the group tries to untangle the human knot until everyone is stood in a chain (if possible).

Human cradle

This exercise must be done with a physically able, confident and trusting group – no fewer than ten people.

Good for	Experiencing new sensations. Developing trust. Creating responsibility. Encouraging safe touch.
What to do	One person agrees to be lifted and then lies on the floor. Everyone else crouches down around the person and places both hands underneath her/his body. Then slowly and carefully they lift the body into the air above their heads if possible, with all hands supporting underneath. Everyone moves together in a group to transport the person across the room. Lower the person very carefully back to the floor.

Musical mimes

Good for	Concentration. Creativity. Fun.
Equipment	Cassette or record player. Music cassettes or records.
What to do	Participants sit or stand in a circle. One person's name is called and they stand in the middle. Whilst the music is playing s/he does one physical action which the rest of the group copy. Change the person in the middle after an agreed time, or when the piece of music ends.
Development	A wide range of music can be used, and can be suggested, chosen or brought in by members of the group.
Variation	People make the music by singing or playing instruments.

The hats game

Good for Co-operation.
Co-ordination.
Memory.
Courage.

Equipment Three different hats.
Music.

What to do Stand or sit in a circle. When the music is played the three hats are passed round from head to head. When the music stops the group decides what action goes with each hat and then the person wearing the hat does that action. The music then starts again. The game goes on until everyone has had a go.

What are we?

Good for Developing trust.
Self-awareness.

What to do Each member of the group must make a statement about being a human being to an alien from outer space,

e.g.: 'We have two arms and two legs.'
'We can talk and sing.'
'We eat food.'

Development The statements can become more personal so that each member relates something specific about her/himself.

How I've changed

Good for Getting to know people.
Self-awareness.

What to do Each group member makes a statement about a change in their lives,

e.g.: 'I used to be frightened of the dark, but now I'm not.'
'I used to worry about my hairstyle, but then I had it cut in a style I really like.'

Development	Group members talk about a change in their lives that they would like to happen.

Guided walk

Good for	Developing trust. Responsibility for others. Fun.
Equipment	Blindfolds, chairs, bags, tables, etc. to provide obstacles.
What to do	Set up an obstacle course. Group members form pairs and one in each is blindfolded. The other person has to guide the 'blind' one around the obstacle course without talking. The roles are then reversed.

Parcels

Good for	Developing listening skills. Getting to know people.
What to do	Tell the group that an imaginary parcel has arrived for each of them. It contains anything in the world that would make them happy. Each member tells the rest of the group what is in her/his box and why it would make her/him happy.
Development	Members share an incident from the previous week that has made them happy. They describe what it is like to feel happy.

Friends

Good for	Boosting self-esteem. Enhancing relationships.
What to do	Ask the group to choose an imaginary friend, then finish the statements: 'My friend is...' (what friend is like) 'I like this friend because...'

Development	Group members talk about friends they have, what they do together and why they like them.

Pass the parcel

Good for	Concentration. Fun. Discussion afterwards.
What to do	Stand in a circle, with one group member in the middle. A 'parcel' (anything will do) has to be passed around the group, but behind their backs, out of sight. The person in the middle must try to guess who has the parcel. When the guess is correct the person in the middle swaps places with that person and the game continues.
Development	Discussion about times when people have been unjustly accused of doing something or when they have been trying to hide something that they feel they should not be doing.

Points of contact

Good for	Developing group co-operation. Practising numerical skills. Developing balance, gross motor skills.
You will need	A large group of people. A large space.
What to do	The group divides into groups of three, four or five. The leader calls out a number and each group have to have that many points of contact on the floor, using feet, hands, etc.
Variation	Can be made competitive. The fastest group to do it gets a point, or the group to hold their stance the longest wins.

Funny faces

Good for	Having fun – a good shared laugh! Breaking the ice. Developing expression.

What to do	The group stands in a circle and the leader starts by making a face as s/he turns to the person next to her/him.
	That person imitates the face as best they can. Then s/he changes the face to something else, turning to the person on her/his other side. And so the sequence continues.

On the soap box

Good for	Developing listening skills. Enhancing self-esteem. Imagination.
You will need	A circle of chairs.
What to do	A group member creates a story, e.g., 'You have been invited from all over the country to attend a meeting of famous explorers. You are especially invited because each of you has discovered something special.'
	Each person describes her/his special discovery and talks about it, giving it a name, etc.
Variation	The leader makes up various scenarios, e.g., a meeting of wizards, photographers, actors.

Silence is golden

Good for	Developing concentration. Developing listening skills. Developing fine motor skills.
You will need	A tambourine.
What to do	Everyone sits quietly in a circle fairly close together. A tambourine is passed from person to person. Everyone tries to avoid any sound being made.

Lighthouse

Good for	Developing sensory-motor co-ordination. Concentration. Team-building. Trust.
You will need	A group of eight people or more. A large space. A tambourine or something similar.
What to do	The group chooses one person to be a lighthouse (the holder of the tambourine). Another person is a ship and is blindfolded. Others in the group position themselves around the room and remain stationary, as rocks in the sea. The blindfolded person (the ship) begins at the edge of the room, moving towards the sound of the lighthouse, who is in the middle of the group shaking the tambourine. If the ship comes near to a rock, the rocks have to clap to warn of danger, guiding the ship towards the lighthouse.

End of the rainbow

Good for	Understanding the needs and wishes of others. Developing listening skills. Creating autonomy of thought processes and memory.
You will need	Pens and paper.
What to do	In pairs people talk about something they really wish for, e.g., 'to be Queen for a day'. All swap round in the group until everyone has shared everyone else's wishes. Come together as a large group and each person in turn tries to recall someone else's wish.
Variation	Everyone writes, or is helped to write, a wish down. All are put in a box and read out at random.

What's good about me?

Good for	Making people think about themselves, reinforcing good points. Telling other people, 'I'm alright!'

In a group or in pairs, (whichever seems the most suitable), one person tells the others what s/he can do, or what is good about her/him; e.g., kindness, always tidy, nice hair, etc.

Variation In pairs, people say what is good about the other person.

Everyone can join in – unless it is obvious the balance would be too uneven.

What do I think about ...?

Good for Expressing thoughts in a setting where they are valued.
Stimulating thoughts, discussion.
Being listened to.
Vocabulary use.

What to do Each person raises a topic of interest to her/him and tells the group about it.

Variation One topic is set for the whole group.
Comments can be made informally.
Comments can be made in turn.

'Things I hate'
'People I hate'
'Things I love'
'People I love' } public figures, characters in film, TV etc.

Call them names

Good for Relieving tension.
Encouraging thought and imagination.
Speaking up.

What to do Ask each person to give an adjective (where possible) to the person next to them, e.g., 'Funny Mary'. The word should describe that person.

Variation The 'calling' word begins with the same letter, e.g., 'Merry Mary'.
Each person can call her/himself something.

67

Good or bad

Good for   Opening up the group.
Giving to the group.
Sharing with others.

What to do   Each person takes a turn to say how s/he feels.

Variation   The person can say why s/he feels as s/he does.

Everyone can speak about one good thing that has happened to her/him that day, or if it is more important to her/him, s/he can speak about a bad thing.

Other members can offer comments as turns are taken.

Role-plays

Good for   Losing inhibitions.
Re-enacting real experience safely.
Understanding another's point of view.
Distancing from difficult subjects.
Introducing embarrassing problems easily as it is more impersonal than discussion.
Giving others the opportunity to make comments and be involved, without necessarily speaking in an obvious way about themselves.

What to do   Set up role-plays about social situations; e.g., being talked about, interrupting, joining in conversations, disagreeing without falling out, public situations, sexual harassment, how to say 'No', how to be treated normally in public surroundings.
The worker may have to help with many of these.

Variation   Devise a longer play with the group to develop a situation.
Develop short plays about emotions like anger and frustration.

Winding down

Good for	Extending the benefits of group work into the individual domain and keeping a sense of one's own importance.
1. *What to do*	Sit in a relaxed position in a circle with body 'grounded', i.e. feet on floor, hands together. Stay quiet for a minute, then take a long, deep breath in and let it out slowly.
	In turn, make a statement of intention – something to work at before the next meeting. It should be practical, to do with attitude or with people. It must be something to help with self-esteem or an opportunity for self-advocacy – and it must be possible!
Variation	The leader can write the intentions down for 'playback'. Each person's 'intent' is written rather than spoken.
2. *What to do*	In a circle, each person finishes the session by telling the group what s/he got out of the session.
Variation	Tell the group what difference the session will make to their approach outside.
3. *What to do*	Each person tells the group something good about her/himself.
Variation	Members tell others what benefit they gained from another person.

Initiating a self-advocacy group

I was invited to initiate self-advocacy sessions by a voluntarily run group comprising two organisers and eight members at a casual drop-in centre for people with learning disabilities, physical disabilities and/or mental health problems.

First session of our newly formed self-advocacy group

Introduction I introduced myself to the group and thanked them for inviting me to help them start their own work towards self-advocacy. I explained that I saw my role initially to weld the group together into a strong team, thus increasing their ability to support each other in whatever changes they wanted to initiate.

Rounds I asked the group to pair off and talk to each other about the things that they presently liked in their lives. Each member then had to introduce her/his partner to the group and relate one thing which that person liked.

The aim of this exercise was to help people relax and listen to each other, to create a feeling of safety and to establish good things they have in common.

I then continued with an open discussion on, 'Things we like and enjoy', followed by a round of 'One thing I'm fed up with now!' At the start of the round I introduced the idea of a 'talking object', such as a conch shell, which is passed around each member of the group in turn and which, when held, allows them to speak. Any member can opt to 'pass' if s/he does not want to contribute to the round.

Responses 'I'm fed up because I don't want to go on a trip being organised by the Day Centre.'

'I'm fed up because I'm having trouble with a neighbour.'

'I'm fed up with being treated like a child because I'm in a wheelchair.'

'I'm fed up with not being able to say "No" to people in case I ruin the relationship.'

'I'm fed up with not being able to say when I feel angry.'

I explained to the group that as they were being honest with each other and trusting the other members with personal problems we may like to have a further round of 'I want to be in this group because...'

They decided to do the round.

Responses   'I want to be in this group because I'm lonely.'

'I want to be in this group because I'm depressed.'

'I want to be in this group because I'm blind, but I still want to help other people.'

'I want to be in this group to learn how to stand up for myself.'

Pairs   I asked the group to return to their pairs and discuss with each other one thing they had achieved and one target they would like to aim for. They then reported these to the group.

Responses | *Achievement* | 'I am working in a hospital now.' |
Target	'I want to be less shy.'
Achievement	'I am helping others and thinking less about my own problems.'
Target	'I want to get rid of my depression.'
Achievement	'Looking after my friends and helping them.'
Target	'I want more time to do things I want to do.'
Achievement	'I have learned to walk.'
Target	'I want to carry on being more independent.'

Ending ritual   Using the couch we each said one thing we got out of today's meeting.

Responses   'It was good to meet nice people.'

'I like being brave.'

'I like making some time for me to think properly.'

Second session of our newly formed self-advocacy group

Introduction

I briefly recapped on the previous session, how we had been honest and trusting with each other. As the members had enjoyed the meeting and returned for another, I suggested they may like to formulate a 'contract' of guidelines on how they wanted to act towards one another in the future. I wrote their suggestions onto a flipchart and together we worked out what they would like to include in their contract. All members subsequently signed it.

Contract

As a group, we would like to carry on being supportive and helpful.

We would like to feel this is a safe place to share problems.

We trust everyone not to talk about our personal problems outside the group.

We would like to listen to each other and not step in unless asked.

We would like each person to have a turn – but they may choose not to and we will understand.

We would like to learn: how to make some changes in our lives, e.g.,
> How to say, 'No.'
> How to change other people's behaviour towards us.
> How to express our feelings and ideas.

If anything else comes up we would also like to deal with it.

We will meet four Mondays in a row:
> from 10.00 – 11.00 am (definite)

We will then decide if we want to continue.

Signed: ....

Communication skills

As a group we then looked at the skills necessary for good communication.

Round   'One thing that has proved difficult this week was...'
                and
          'One thing that I enjoyed this week was...'

Asking for change

Each group member volunteered a change they wanted to s/he in her/his life.

Response   Kerry wanted to change her mother's attitude towards her. This was too vague so I asked her to focus on one aspect and she decided that she wanted to deal with the way in which her mother nagged her to get up in the morning.

By using role-play with another group member playing her mother, Kerry was able to explore and find the best way of responding to this nagging without provoking further negative attitudes.

Throughout this activity everyone was highly supportive and listened well. They then helped each other decide on targets to achieve the changes they wanted.

Asking others to change

Using the following questions:

◆ What is the behaviour that upsets you? (make it brief and specific)
◆ How does this behaviour make you feel?
◆ What is the actual change you want the person to consider? (make it a small change to start with)

We then wrote or asked others to write a short script based on the three point plan.

Response   Sarah was worried about her mother's illness and the tablets she was taking.

> **Her target was to get in touch with her mother's doctor and discuss her anxieties with him.**

Cathy did not get on with her neighbours and was irritated by their overgrown hedge blocking out her light.

> **Her target was to approach them calmly and ask if they would trim the hedge.**

Ending ritual

We decided we'd like to end this session with a round of thanking people. Using our couch we each thanked the group for something.

Responses   'I'd like to thank you for listening to me.'

'Thank you for not getting impatient.'

'Thank you for helping me with my problem.'

Personal accounts – a worker's perspective

Harry – the story so far

Harry, the youngest of three children (all of whom still live at home), is 25 years old. Before coming to the Centre he was working on a voluntary basis for a small family firm in a nearby town. His duties included sweeping up, making tea, washing up and walking the dogs.

To get to work Harry paid his own bus fare. This was quite a considerable amount out of what appeared to be very little family income. The whole family were either on benefit or in low-paid employment.

One of our first tasks was to check up on his benefit entitlement. Harry came to us two days a week and continued to work the other three days. The question of whether he should be paying his bus fare as well as being unpaid for the work he did was raised with the people for whom he worked. Despite the fact that they said they valued his work they were unwilling to make any contribution towards the travelling costs. Eventually Harry and his family decided he should give up working for them. Harry did not have a social worker but was seen occasionally by a community nurse.

When he first arrived at the Centre, Harry was not used to being treated as an adult. He spent most of his time trying to make people laugh at his slapstick antics and jokes, or creeping up behind people and shouting '**Boo!**'

Within his family Harry seemed to take on the role of clown. On the one hand he made them laugh, but was then chastised for being 'daft'. He always needed to ask permission before embarking on any task, however obvious or simple. He seemed capable of completing most tasks alone, but lacked the confidence to initiate anything himself.

Joining the self-advocacy process

Harry's introduction to personal development groups at the Centre came when he joined the drama therapy sessions. He found the idea of sitting in a circle listening to other people, and in turn being listened to, quite difficult. He was fidgety and could not make eye contact. He spoke very quietly, in monosyllables, and raised his hands to his head and face whilst speaking. His diction was very poor. During the preliminary 'newsround' he remembered little of what he had done during the week and therefore made little contribution to the conversation. During role-play and drama structures Harry found it very hard not to break the atmosphere with jokey and inappropriate comments.

A feature of our work within this group was for people (if they wished) to carry a 'diary' in which to make notes of forthcoming events, record achievements they had experienced recently, or just to make positive remarks about their life generally. At the front of every book was a passage which emphasised that it was the property of the individual, should only be written in at her/his request, that all entries must be positive and where possible the owner should determine what was written.

Harry seemed to like this idea and wanted one. In fact the next week he brought in his own notebook. The use of this diary brought about two obvious changes: Harry now had a legitimate reason to approach people to gain their attention; and when he saw what people were writing about, he came to recognise the positive qualities that others saw in him.

About this time, Harry decided to join the Goal-Achieving Group. This group was a variation on the theme of 'problem-solving'. The name enabled us to look more positively at getting things done, rather than at putting things right. It also meant we could break down the tasks into small achievable weekly goals.

People appeared comfortable with ideas such as finding a telephone number, speaking to one person about difficulties, asking a question of their key worker, etc. It proved very popular and as individuals became more confident, so the tasks became more complex, or we would combine two small tasks to be completed in a shorter period of time. In this way the tasks were built upon, week by week, leading eventually to a 'goals achieved' group celebration.

Initially group members were asked to make a list of all their ambitions, all the things they really wanted in life. Harry had a list of seven or eight items. The main one was to be a trolley-collector at the local supermarket. He was quite concerned about telling other people outside the group; he felt they would not let him take on such a job.

Our first task then was to decide who needed to know. He had an IP coming up soon and if he was to at least try for the job the question had to be raised at that meeting. Harry wanted to speak to his keyworker first. Together they raised the question at his IPP.

He was put in touch with the Skills & Opportunities Project. Having received such a positive response from the people at his meeting Harry also made enquiries at the supermarket himself.

They promised to let him know as soon as a vacancy occurred. Within a few weeks Harry was working part-time at his chosen occupation. Far from responding negatively, his family seemed proud of him and went to great expense to buy the trousers and shoes he had to have as part of his uniform.

Of his seven or eight original ambitions Harry had achieved at least five. He no longer needs to use his diary to the same extent, but always carries it with him. He is very responsible and always asks for entries to be made in it whenever he perceives a positive experience has occurred. He very rarely needs to borrow a pen and has never forgotten or lost the diary. He no longer comes to the Goal-Achieving Group because he is now out at work with a DIY group. He still attends the drama sessions. He still likes to have a laugh and joke but these are now much more appropriate and he is also able to hold mature and meaningful conversations.

Considerations

For me, the worker I had to bolster Harry's confidence in the initial stages by encouraging self-esteem. It took time to persuade him to make the first move of talking to people outside the safety of the group. I feel Harry expressed himself so openly because he felt valued within our group. His ambition was very important to him and he needed to trust us with it. If his idea had not been so well received by others I would have had to persuade the sceptics to take his request seriously. The most important implication for myself as a worker was, however, to be prepared to let him move on and recognise his readiness to leave the group.

For Harry Harry had to take his courage in both hands and declare his wishes to people who appeared to have control of his life. He had to approach people in a calm and mature way. He had to be prepared to follow through decisions he had made for himself.

He had to learn to take criticism (he was sometimes told off at work for not having his hair cut), and respond positively. He had to act on instructions and take the consequences of his actions.

For his family Harry's family had to recognise him as an adult and be aware that he should not be treated as their 'baby' or a naughty little boy. They had to accept that he was able to make decisions for himself and that these decisions had to be taken seriously. In practical terms they had to allow him to travel independently to and from the town. His lifestyle changed radically as he achieved more and more of his ambitions. He became a very sociable character who mixed more than any other member of his family. This meant he often arrived home late at night. They also saw and acknowledged that other people valued Harry and the contribution he was making. This was quite a challenge to them.

Andrew – the story so far

Andrew, aged 33, had lived in a hostel for ten years, attending the local centre daily. The established pattern was of going home to spend the weekend with his parents once a month. A driver picked up Mum and Dad in Smithtown, brought them to Maintown to collect Andrew and took them all back to Smithtown. At the end of the weekend the process was reversed. The arrangements were made between staff and parents and Andrew had no say in what happened.

Andrew moved to a small, family-run private establishment about 15 miles from Maintown but nearer to Smithtown. The Day Centre was also 15 miles away which meant an early start to the day, but Andrew did not have to go and he chose instead two weekly sessions at a small local centre.

The former arrangements for weekends continued. He had good personal care skills, but whenever he returned from his parents he expected to be dressed and washed. He relayed messages from his parents about what he should eat. He argued with the other residents and he had a rash on his face. Each time these things lasted for up to a week.

Joining the self-advocacy process

After four months he started to make excuses not to go away for the weekend and expected his carers, David and Jane, to tell his parents. David and Jane noticed these events, discussed them and fed back to Andrew what they saw and what they thought about it.

Initially they helped him by telling his parents what Andrew wanted them to say by phone and in writing. They asked me, as an independent third party, to mediate as they felt that his parents would assume that these ideas were being put into his head and were not his own wishes.

He wanted to see his parents, but not every month as he did not want to miss out on what was happening in his new home while he was away. He decided that he would visit them four times a year – at Easter, Christmas, for his birthday and in the summer. He had always felt humiliated by his parents chaperoning him on visits to their house and he now wanted to have some control over what happened to him.

He felt torn as there were vastly different expectations of him in different places. This was fed back to David and Jane and to Andrew's parents who could also express their feelings and views.

Andrew's wish to have some control over his life, to be the person he wanted to be, and particularly to enjoy his new freedom to experiment with making choices, led to conflict between Andrew, his sister and parents, and between David and Jane and his sister and parents.

His sister Jill was concerned that by not visiting his parents as often Andrew was cutting himself off from his family and would not want to see Jill, her husband and their young sons. This was exacerbated when Andrew decided not to go to his nephew's birthday party despite (or perhaps because of) intense lobbying from his family.

Jill spoke to David and Jane about this, initially angry but later with more understanding. I took Andrew to visit Jill. Eventually common ground was reached in that it was accepted that Andrew was enjoying his first opportunity to experiment with making choices for himself and he (like everyone else) was allowed to make lousy as well as good choices.

Jill felt it was more appropriate for her to explain all of this to their parents from her standpoint of supporting Andrew. She underlined this by offering Andrew an open invitation to visit her whenever he wanted to.

Andrew visited his parents for a weekend in the summer. David took him and I picked him up, avoiding the opportunity for his parents to make the arrangements. He has not wanted to visit them at home since, but at Christmas he arranged to spend a day with Jill when his parents were there. At his last personal meeting (review of IPP) Andrew decided not to invite his parents and he distributed the notes of the meeting to whom he wished.

Considerations

For me, the worker

Helping Andrew was time consuming. It involved many long journeys and working in the evenings.

I needed to plan my work and to think carefully about what Andrew and his carers were asking me to do.

It was important to 'stick to my guns' in supporting Andrew, and not be persuaded to tread a middle line which his parents might have preferred.

I needed to keep checking where Andrew was in all this so that I did not start to make assumptions about his wishes or feelings.

The possibility of a complaint being made by Andrew's parents caused me some anxiety. This and Andrew's obvious strong feelings about the situation made me constantly check, with myself and in supervision, that I was being a good advocate.

For Andrew

He ran the risk of being censured and ridiculed by his parents. He feared his father's anger.

He had to cope with the 'newness' of the situation, i.e. taking responsibility for his own decisions, and with the realisation that some people might be upset and try to influence him.

His feeling of trust in his carers boosted his confidence and his ability to be assertive.

For his carers   They invested a lot of time in supporting Andrew. They earned his trust and encouraged him to speak for himself.

They had to keep checking that what they were doing was what Andrew wanted.

They were confident that the service they were providing was meeting the needs of and was wanted by the people who lived in their hostel.

For his parents   They were shocked that their son was challenging them. For the first time in his life Andrew was not automatically doing what they wanted or expected him to do.

They were forced to look at their own perceptions of what a service should or would provide.

They looked for someone to blame. They felt that someone was putting ideas into Andrew's head. They could accept that his practical skills were improving and increasing, but not his ability and confidence to think things through and make decisions for himself.

Susan – the story so far

Susan, aged 46, returned to live with her parents following a two-year residential further education course. Prior to and during this time she had developed a wide range of interests and had some clear ideas about how she wanted to spend her time, including part-time work, and spending some time at home on her own. Her parents wanted her to be occupied from 9.00 a.m. to 4.00 p.m. for five days each week.

Joining the self-advocacy process

During her time at college Susan had been supported and encouraged to express herself. Consequently she had grown in confidence. Her parents meanwhile viewed this development with apprehension and interpreted her growing confidence as being over-assertive and selfish.

With practical help (introductions to resources, claiming benefits) and support, Susan was able to achieve most of her wants with her parents' co-operation. This involved me in spending time with Susan and her parents (separately and together), encouraging them to talk through their anxieties and frustrations.

Now Susan spends two and a half days at a day centre doing sessions of her own choice, including drama, woodwork and work preparation skills, using public transport to get there. She often leaves the house after her parents and returns home before them. She occasionally spends a day at home on her own. She is pursuing opportunities for doing voluntary work.

Considerations

For me, the worker   Working with Susan and her family took up a lot of time. There were visits with Susan to resources, dealing with practicalities (claiming benefits, arranging transport), phone calls from, and visits to parents to discuss their anxieties.

As the 'front person' for Social Services I felt embarrassed and frustrated by the system's shortcomings.

I felt invigorated and spurred on by Susan's obvious pleasure in spending her time how she chose.

I had to check constantly, through my supervision sessions, that the way I was working was appropriate, that I was helping Susan to develop her chosen lifestyle and also supporting her parents through this phase of transition.

For Susan   She had to prove herself to her parents by showing, for example, that she was capable of locking the door when leaving the house, that she knew her way around town, that her behaviour was grown-up, that she helped with housework and went on family trips, but that she also liked time alone. This was frustrating and humiliating at times.

She had to 'stick to her guns', to decide what she wanted and to go for it. Sometimes she was described as 'stroppy'.

She also showed she could compromise by deciding which things she would concede on. By doing this she often made extra gains later.

For her parents They had to recognise and deal with their anxieties, which were largely about not knowing how capable Susan was and underestimating her. They wanted to protect her.

There was some conflict with Susan, especially when they wanted to provide transport everywhere and supervise her friendships.

They experienced frustration with Social Services on different levels. I would not support their wish for traditional five day a week care in a training centre. Services took time to set up, from referral, to visits, to an offer of a place, to discussing which sessions Susan wanted to take up. Initially transport provided was unreliable.

Diana – the story so far

Diana, aged 22, very shy and attractive, had always lived at home with parents and three younger siblings. For more than two years Diana had felt unhappy at home because of teasing by her younger brothers and family financial difficulties. She had been troubled by lack of money for her and lack of care.

This family background had done nothing to boost her confidence and she seemed very 'stuck'. Her parents did not want her to move out, but did not take very good care of or show much interest in her. Diana was not allowed to cook, use electricity except for the radio, shop or travel on her own. No one had time to support her while she did these things or learned to do them for herself. From her programme at the Centre it was obvious that there was undeveloped potential.

Joining the self-advocacy process

Diana began to talk about moving out after listening to many of her group who were either interested or had recently made the change. Independent Living Skills sessions, discussions in groups and with me gave Diana more knowledge.

She began to help the less able in her key group and had special attention from her key worker to help her build confidence – taking charge of keys, money, books, a wheelchair, etc.

Very soon, all these responsibilities were carried out competently. Diana was often able to remind others what they had forgotten.

Diana and I had long conversations about the possibility of moving out and in particular about the expected opposition from her family. Getting a voluntary job outside the Centre was another boost to her confidence and eventually Diana agreed that the resettlement officer be informed of her wish to move to a group home.

When this happened, the officer agreed to speak for Diana as she was not taken seriously at home. The outcome was not pleasant as the mother did not wish Diana to leave. The father was never available to talk but we were told he was also against the move. It was obviously going to be a difficult time for Diana. At another meeting I was included and the meeting appeared to go well, although Diana never once looked at her mother. Afterwards, the message from the home was that the professionals were just trying to fill places, to push Diana out, to take her away from home. There was verbal abuse over the phone.

After some months a place became free and there was a chance for Diana to move out. Unfortunately, someone else 'won' the place, so there was disappointment and more abuse. The next chance came, and Diana got in. The actual move was very awkward but she has settled in well and visits her family. The relationship with her brothers is much improved, and the parents are getting used to the change. Diana has integrated well into the Group Home and is gaining in confidence and self-esteem all the time.

Considerations

For me, the worker   This was quite a long process and it was difficult to keep a steady input going for Diana.

I was concerned that she really did want to leave and that I was not reading into her few words what I thought should happen.

I was worried that we might 'push' too hard.

I was affected adversely by the verbal abuse when I thought I was doing the right thing.

I was worried that the move might fail and Diana would regress. Another move would be even more difficult.

For Diana   There was a risk of abuse at home.

Diana had to be brave and keep steady in her views whilst being worried about what exactly a move might bring.

Diana risked not being 'chosen' for a place for a long time.

Diana took the responsibility on for herself.

The support from the workers was very important.

For her parents   Diana was unexpectedly doing something herself. While at home she had mostly done little but spend time in her room, away from the family.

They would miss her financial contribution.

They would miss her, their eldest child.

They blamed the workers, as they did not view Diana as capable of making decisions for herself.

Moira – the story so far

Moira (45), lived in a local authority hostel for people with learning disabilities for a number of years. Previously she had from an early age been resident in a locked ward in a psychiatric hospital, where she had exhibited bizarre behaviours and become quite uncontrollable.

Her move into the hostel had helped to lessen these behaviours but she still developed some common institutional practices such as eating meals as quickly as possible. She would sometimes appear to be very devious and staff working with her would often suspect her of being 'up to something'. If she was put under any sort of pressure, sometimes just by being asked to do a job in the hostel, she could be very moody and stubborn, often shouting and storming out of the room.

All of Moira's leisure activities were shared with the other residents of the hostel. Their trips out were in large groups and their holidays were spent together at a holiday camp. Moira did not have the opportunity to make any individual choice about her day-to-day activities.

Moira also attended a large day centre where I worked as her key worker. There her day-time activities were as part of large groups and her choice of activities was limited.

With the development of group homes in the last five years, Moira had witnessed several of her friends moving into the community to live with three or four other people. She expressed an interest to do the same to her carers at the hostel, who told her that unless her behaviour improved she had no hope of moving.

She was promised that she would be put on a waiting list for moving if she demonstrated a considerable improvement in her behaviour. Each time she became upset and was violent in any way, she jeopardised her chance of moving.

Joining the self-advocacy process

Moira slowly began to try really hard to conform to the requirements as set down by the staff at the hostel. She moved within the hostel to a smaller group and underwent a training programme to develop her independent living skills.

Because of her history of behaviour, it seemed to me that Moira had doubly to prove herself to be worthy of consideration for a group home. She had an awful lot to overcome in convincing her carers to give her a chance at moving out. When places came up, it seemed that other people always got the first choice. It was as if no one could believe she would succeed.

Finally, after a long struggle, Moira's wishes were recognised and she was considered for a group home. A lodgings officer who had been invited to her annual review considered Moira's situation and suggested lodgings might be more suitable in meeting her needs. A landlady was found and an initial visit was made. The landlady and her husband had three children who had left home. Their house was in the country on a farm estate where the husband worked as a farmhand.

It was obvious that Moira liked the set-up and was very excited about a weekend visit. Over several months, more visits were arranged and there seemed to be a likelihood of a successful placement.

A move was finally agreed and Moira's whole personality seemed to change. She became bubbly and excited as opposed to rather grumpy. She was helpful and positive as opposed to objectionable.

After being in the supported lodgings for several months, her moods were still positive and she was pleasant company. She seemed to be delighted with her new situation and the landlady seemed happy too.

I recognised a definite change in Moira's manner and attitude to life. She began to smile a lot and she was obviously really enjoying life. She was always pleased to see me and there was no evidence of her previous difficult behaviours. She talked about saving money for a holiday and she had been out choosing new clothes. Her general appearance was pleasing.

After several months in the new accommodation, I was asked to set up a review to involve all parties in Moira's move to establish that all was well. It came to light that there had been 'undercurrent grumblings' about whether Moira was particularly happy. This had come from a staff member at the hostel who was close to Moira and seemed to be questioning if the placement was right for her. It appeared that Moira had seen the carer once or twice and had gone running to her with open arms, saying 'I miss you.' The carer, it seemed, was interpreting this as, 'I'm unhappy and want to come back to the hostel'. I thought it meant, 'Hello, I've moved and I'm really happy, but I do miss you.'

I agreed that we did need to check that everything was going smoothly, but I also thought that the staff member's attitude could have really put Moira's placement in jeopardy. It was very disempowering, almost suggesting that Moira had failed, as expected.

Considerations

For me, the worker

I had to believe in Moira, have faith in her decisions, and support her convincingly at times when she was being doubted.

I had to support Moira and try to see things from her point of view so that I did not collude with others against her best interests.

I had to encourage Moira to continue to be a self-advocate and help her to grow and develop her potential.

I had to support her landlady actively by showing an interest in Moira's life and offering my help when it was needed.

I had to feedback my thoughts to Moira's former staff to assure them that they had worked well with her, and she had made the right move.

For Moira

Her ability to cope and adapt may always be doubted and she needs to be prepared for this.

One big success is bound to boost her confidence and she will then begin asking for other things.

Other people might overestimate her ability and lay on her expectations that are too great.

More opportunities for developing her individual tastes and interests will come her way. She will need to get used to having more options and decisions to make, e.g., where to go on holiday.

For the staff

They had to come to terms with the sense of loss they felt as a result of someone they were fond of moving away.

They had to accept that Moira had made a big step towards independence and does not rely on them for support any more.

They had to be prepared to take risks, even if they thought a plan may not work out. There will always be an element of uncertainty but they had to allow Moira to finally decide her own future.

They had to be prepared to continue to support Moira and view her decision to move positively. If it does not work out, they should not say, 'I told you so.'

Resources and useful addresses

Below is a list of resources and addresses that we have come across and found useful. We are very conscious that there are many excellent books and organisations that we have not mentioned.

Resources

Learning disabilities

Beginning to Listen, D. Brandon and J. Ridley, MIND (1983), CMH, 1985.
> Do people with learning disabilities like living in special homes or hostels or would they prefer to live independently with a proper job? The authors have thoroughly researched the question by talking to a group of people from a hostel for adults with learning disabilities. The conclusion of the study shows that people with learning disabilities have very strong views on how they would like their lives to be.

Know Me As I Am, An Anthology of Prose, Poetry and Art by People with Learning Difficulties, D. Atkinson and F. Williams, (ed.), Hodder and Stoughton, 1990.

An Ordinary Day, S. Dowson, CMH, 1988.
> This report describes days in the lives of people with learning disabilities, encouraging awareness of what it is like to live with a physical or mental disability.

Our Mutual Handicap, P. Williams, CMH.
> The author of this book is challenging the way people assume those with disabilities think and view the world.

Self-esteem

The Antecedents of Self-Esteem, R. Coopersmith, Freeman, 1967.
Coopersmith has developed a very easy to use self-esteem questionnaire.

Improving Self-Esteem and Reading, D. Lawrence, Volume 27, No. 3 Educational Research, 1985.
Lawrence has done pioneering work in the field of self-esteem with children and has written many articles and books on the subject.

Self Concept Development and Education, R. Burns, Holt Saunders, 1982.
A thorough survey of all research relating to self concept theory and practice in education.

Towards a State of Esteem, California State Department of Education, 1990.
This is the final report of the California Task Force which was set up to promote self-esteem and personal social responsibility.

101 Ways to Boost Self Concept, Canfield and Wells, Prentice Hall, 1978.

101 Ways to Enhance Self Concept in the Classroom, A Handbook for Teachers, Counsellors and Group Leaders, Boston, Allyn and Bacon, 1994.

101 Ways to Develop Student Self-Esteem and Responsibility, Canfield and Siccone, Boston, Allyn and Bacon, 1993.
Very readable compilations of excellent practical ideas to initiate with young people.

Self-advocacy

Developing Self-Advocacy Skills, M. Clare, Further Education Unit, 1990.
The result of a project carried out by the East Midlands Further Education Council, the book includes the experiences of key workers who were trained and supported by the author. It is

aimed at anyone committed to improving standards for people with learning disabilities, offering advice to those already involved and help for those about to begin.

The Growing Voice, B. Crawley, VIA, 1988.
Illustrates how opportunities for self-advocacy for people with learning disabilities is increasing with services provided for them. The results are compiled from a questionnaire distributed to every Adult Training Centre, Social Education Centre and Hospital, and Hospital for Mental Health, in England, Wales and Scotland between 1986 and 1987. The booklet contains the precise, factual information for anyone interested in the study of self-advocacy.

Learning About Self-Advocacy, Booklets 1–5, B. Crawley, J. Mills, A. Wertheimer, A. Whittaker, P. Williams and J. Billis, CMH, (now VIA), 1988.
These booklets are simply and clearly written for people wishing to have a say in the way their lives go.

Self-Advocacy at Work Portfolio, EMFEC.
This pack seeks to offer chances for people involved in services to look at, and possibly change their own attitudes and practice. The portfolio includes a handbook containing six modules: the context of self-advocacy; what is self-advocacy; challenging power; self-advocacy through groups and self-advocacy through preparing portfolios. There is also an audio cassette and a number of A3 sheets, covering a variety of subjects.

Sticking Up for Yourself – Self-advocacy and people with learning difficulties, K. Simons, Norah Fry Research Centre, 1993.
The author visited three different self-advocacy groups from Somerset and Avon, talking to staff and group members asking them what they think of the services provided and how they feel about their lives.

We Can Change the Future, D. Cooper and J. Hersov, National Bureau for Handicapped Students, 1988.
The book is divided into modules, with clear advice to help self-advocates and those working with them.

We Can Speak for Ourselves, P. Williams and B. Shoultz, Indiana University Press, 1984.
> Written by people with learning disabilities, this book tells the story of self-advocacy projects.

Group work

Working More Creatively With Groups, J. F. Benson, Tavistock Publications (1987) Routledge, 1991.
> A practical guide for anyone involved in organising group sessions. The book is suitable for both the experienced and inexperienced worker dealing with planning and successful group leading.

The Red Book of Groups, G. Houston, F. C. Barnwell, 1987, (2nd Edition).
> Suitable for anyone involved in leading a supportive group who would like to improve their skills, the book contains likely scenarios and how to deal with them.

Related topics

Chance to Choose, Hilary Dixon, LDA, 1992. (First published, 1988 as *Sexuality and Mental Handicap*)
> Contains all the information you will need to cover such subjects as body awareness, relationships, being sexual and pregnancy. It offers a scheme of work, practical activities, lesson plans and resources.

Creative Drama in Groupwork, S. Jennings, Winslow Press, 1986.
> The book outlines how to lead effective, enjoyable and rewarding drama lessons and contains over 150 games and activities.

Creative Games in Groupwork, R. Dynes, Winslow Press, 1990.
> The book contains a number of games, organised into sections with games of a similar theme, (e.g., quiet and noisy).

Creative Movement in Dance, H. Payne, Winslow Press, 1990.
This book contains 180 activities for creative movement and dance. Each activity is accompanied by a sample session and precise guidelines.

Developing Friendships, A. Richardson and J. Ritchie, Pinters Publishers Ltd. 1989.
The book helps and encourages people with learning disabilities to live independently and make their own friendships. It also helps those who help and care for them to increase their understanding.

Going to Work, A. Wertheimer, employment opportunities for people with mental handicaps in Washington State, USA, 1985.
The report takes a brief look at five schemes where handicapped people were being trained and supported in paid employment.

Useful addresses

British Institute of Learning Difficulties (BILD)
Information and Resource Centre
Wolverhampton Road
Kidderminster
Worcs DY10 3PD
Tel: 0562 850251

Citizen Advocacy Information and Training
Unit 2R Leroy House
436 Essex Road
London N1 3QP
Tel: 071 359 8289

Creative Young People Together (CRYPT)
Forum Stirling Road
Chichester
West Sussex PO19 2EN
Tel: 0243 786064

EMFEC
Robins Wood House
Robins Wood Road
Aspley
Nottingham NG8 3NH
Tel: 0602 293291

King's Fund Centre
126 Albert Street
London NW1 7NF
Tel: 071 267 6111

National Bureau for Handicapped Studies (NBHS)
336 Brixton Road
London SW9 7AA
Tel: 071 274 0565

National Council for Voluntary Organisations
Regent's Wharf
8 All Saints Street
London N1 9RL
Tel: 071 713 6161

The National Institute of
Adult Continuing Education (NIACE)
198 De Montford Street
Leicester LE1 7GE
Tel: 0533 551 451

The Norah Fry Research Centre
University of Bristol
3 Priary Road
Bristol BS8 1TX
Tel: 0272 238137

People First
Instrument House
207–215 Kings Cross Road
London WC1X 9DD
Tel: 071 713 6400

Values Into Action (VIA)
Oxford House
Derbyshire Street
London E2 6HG
Tel: 071 729 5436